5-Day Spanish Verb Power Challenge

All the Shortcuts You Need to Speak Spanish

Linda van der Hoeven

© **Copyright 2022 - All rights reserved.**

The content contained within this book may not be reproduced, duplicated or transmitted without direct written permission from the author or the publisher.

Under no circumstances will any blame or legal responsibility be held against the publisher, or author, for any damages, reparation, or monetary loss due to the information contained within this book, either directly or indirectly.

Legal Notice:

This book is copyright protected. It is only for personal use. You cannot amend, distribute, sell, use, quote or paraphrase any part, or the content within this book, without the consent of the author or publisher.

Disclaimer Notice:

Please note the information contained within this document is for educational and entertainment purposes only. All effort has been executed to present accurate, up to date, reliable, complete information. No warranties of any kind are declared or implied. Readers acknowledge that the author is not engaged in the rendering of legal, financial, medical or professional advice. The content within this book has been derived from various sources. Please consult a licensed professional before attempting any techniques outlined in this book.

By reading this document, the reader agrees that under no circumstances is the author responsible for any losses, direct or indirect, that are incurred as a result of the use of the information contained within this document, including, but not limited to, errors, omissions, or inaccuracies.

Table of Contents

Introduction	Page 4
Day 1: The 25 Most Used Spanish Verbs	Page 6
Day 2: Use the Future Tense With the Help of 6 Little Words	Page 19
Day 3: How to Form the Stem of the Verb, the Basics of all Conjugations	Page 26
Day 4: Time to Learn the Present Tense. Simple!	Page 40
Day 5: A Simple Trick to Form the Past Tense	Page 54
Final Exercises	Page 61
Conclusion: Where to Go Next?	Page 67
BONUS: Spanish conjugation blueprint	Page 70
References	Page 72

Introduction

Do you want to be able to have fluent conversations in Spanish but don't know where to start? Are traditional lessons hard to put into action right away but you are still determined to speak it? If so, then the *5 Day Spanish Verb Power Challenge* is for you.

One of the best ways to learn a new language is by speaking it with others. Most of us don't notice it but we learned English this way. So, why should any other language be different? Instead of trying to learn grammar, punctuation, or syntax from the beginning, it is better to talk as soon as possible even if the way we talk isn't grammatically correct. After all, no one expects you to speak perfect Spanish immediately.

Having said this, I present to you the challenge: 5 lessons, one per day, that will teach you basic verb conjugations used in real, everyday conversations by native and non-native Spanish speakers alike. Once you've learned everything this guide has to offer, you will have solid grounds to speak Spanish, understand it, and most importantly, continue your journey in learning a new language along the way.

What can you expect from this guide? The aim is to teach you in an easy way some of the most used verbs by Spanish speakers as well as their conjugations in present, past, and future tense, throughout the course of five days. Bear in mind that there are actually 23 different tenses in the Spanish language; however, you won't be learning all of them in this book, just the necessary ones to hold your own in real conversations. We strip everything down to the absolute necessities. A toolbox to have real life conversation in Spanish without being thrown off by the complexity of a language.

And so, the *5 Day Spanish Verb Power Challenge* consists of the following lessons:

1. Day 1: The 25 verbs you must learn to have any conversation in Spanish.
2. Day 2: Use the future tense with the help of 6 little words.
3. Day 3: How to form the stem of the verb, the basics of all conjugations.
4. Day 4: Time to learn the present tense. Simple!
5. Day 5: A simple trick to form the past tense.

Let's start!

Day 1: The 25 Most Used Spanish Verbs

They say the first step is always the most difficult one, even more so when it comes to learning a new language. But you've decided to do it! Let's hit the ground running then with our first lesson.

On this day you will get familiar with some of the most used verbs in Spanish. In terms of memorization, this will be the lesson where you will have to do the most. I know this might be tedious for some, but I assure you once you have a grasp on the meaning of these verbs the rest of the lessons should be a breeze in comparison.

Where to begin? Believe it or not, the Spanish language has around 20,000 different verbs, quite a lot! The good news is no one really knows them all and you don't need to in order to speak Spanish. Like in most languages, some verbs make the foundations of any normal conversation, and today you will be learning 25 verbs which I believe are all you need to get your point across without any problems.

So, with nothing more to add for now, here is the list and what it means in the English language:

Verb in Spanish	Verb in English
Ser	To be (permanent)
Estar	To be (temporarily)
Hacer	To do
Tener	To have
Ir	To go
Hablar	To talk
Coger	To get
Vivir	To live
Traer	To bring
Beber	To drink
Necesitar	To need
Tocar	To touch
Querer	To want
Deber	To must
Poner	To put
Poder	To be able/can
Salir	To go out
Buscar	To search
Encontrar	To find
Dormir	To sleep
Saber	To know
Dar	To give

Trabajar	To work
Comer	To eat
Venir	To come

Before continuing with today's lesson, make sure you have a good understanding of the meaning of these verbs. While it is best you memorize them, you can always come back to this table no matter what day you are on in the challenge. However, I advise that you push yourself, at your own pace, to know these meanings by heart since this is the first step to speaking fluently. To achieve this, here are some ways to help memorize these verbs.

Some Tips for Memorizing

For most of us it is difficult to memorize new words and concepts when all we do is read them again and again. More often than not, this method leads to frustration and desperation. Ultimately, we end up leaving the new thing we are studying. However, some level of frustration is natural when learning anything new and we must power through it. But this process does not necessarily mean you have to brute force your way to success.

Sure, some people find this path to be the best, but if you are not one of them remember that it is valid and even necessary to rest every so often: Take your attention away from the lessons, eat a snack and make sure to hydrate yourself, go for a walk, or just lay down. Once your frustration is gone, you will be able to continue studying with renewed energy and the new things you learn will most likely stick in your mind.

Now that you are back here, I would like to suggest a unique method to learn the 25 verbs above. You probably went at it by reading the verbs in Spanish, and what they mean in English, then you would repeat this until you could recite the list without looking. Finally, you would check which verbs you failed in and reread them. While this is the normal approach, when it comes to verbs, I find that it is not the most effective.

After all, what exactly are verbs? They are words to describe actions, so when learning them it is useful to act out what their meanings are. This way you won't only associate the verbs in Spanish with their English counterparts, you will start to link them with your everyday actions too, making both your brain and body memorize them.

It may seem childish or even useless at first, but studying doesn't have to be all serious to be effective. Acting out the words you are reading will make the task less tedious now that you are adding movement to the mix. I assure you will have more fun memorizing the list like this. However, there is also a hidden purpose in acting the verbs as you read them–Once you put the book down for the day and go about your daily life, you will suddenly remember the verbs whenever you are doing the actions they describe, and the best part is, it will come naturally!

Hopefully, these tips will make memorization a lot easier and, when you know the verbs by heart, one of the hardest parts of the challenge will be complete. Congratulations! The first big hurdle is behind you now. However, our lesson for today doesn't end here. Don't worry though, you won't be doing anymore 'mandatory' memorizing for now. Before continuing you need to be aware of some information about the verbs you've just learned, to make the coming days easier.

Regular and Irregular Verbs

When you were learning English formally you must have heard about regular and irregular verbs. A quick reminder won't do any harm though: A regular verb is a verb that maintains its stem and follows a concrete formula when you are conjugating it in any tense and person, whereas an irregular verb is a verb that changes its stem when you are conjugating it and/or deviates from the formula that applies to regular verbs. For example:

- "To want" is a regular verb, all you have to do to conjugate it is add letters after the stem ie. I want–I wanted, he wants–he wanted, etc.
- "To go" is an irregular verb, you will need to change the stem inorder to conjugate it, especially in the past tenses ie. I go–I went, he goes– he went, etc.

Now that your mind has been refreshed you most likely remembered that what makes a verb regular or irregular is arbitrary, there isn't a concrete rule or method to distinguish between both groups. Instead, we had to learn irregular verbs and their conjugations by heart whenever they came up. This is also the case in the Spanish language.

Don't worry, you won't need to research for yourself which of the 25 verbs in this chapter are regular and which are irregular, I have divided them for you. While it is not critical for you to memorize which verbs go in each group, it's something you will need to know in the future as you continue on your learning journey.

Regular verbs	**Irregular verbs**
Hablar	*Ser*
Vivir	*Estar*
Beber	*Hacer*
Necesitar	*Tener*
Deber	*Ir*
Trabajar	*Coger*
Comer	*Traer*
Tocar	*Querer*
Buscar	*Poner*
	Poder
	Salir
	Encontrar
	Dormir
	Saber
	Dar
	Venir

As you can see, most of the verbs in the list are irregular. This makes their conjugations tricky in different tenses. Unfortunately, you will have to learn each of their forms by heart, but you will have plenty of time to do so as you speak more and more. Besides, thanks to some tricks we will be able to go around some of the conjugations while still speaking Spanish correctly and naturally.

Now, because of this table, it may seem like there are more irregular than regular verbs in Spanish, but this is not the case, so don't be alarmed. For now, though, let's keep your focus on these verbs since we will be using them for the rest of the guide.

Are you still with me? Good! We are almost done with lesson number one. You may be wondering, "what else could there possibly be?" Rest assured that there won't be any more memorizing verbs, however, there are some important things you must know in case you plan on continuing learning Spanish.

Spanish Verbs Are Very Specific

Earlier I said there were around 20,000 verbs in Spanish. While it is pretty much impossible that someone uses even half of these in their lifetime, they reflect just how specific this language can be sometimes. This is one of the main causes of frustration when learning Spanish, most of us will use the wrong verb or form even if what we are saying is grammatically correct. In fact, there are some instances where one verb in English may be replaced by up to three or more verbs in Spanish, depending on the context.

Let's take the verb, "to be" as an example. From the get-go we can see how two different verbs can mean "to be" in Spanish: these are '*ser*' and '*estar.*' However, there will be situations in which you can even use *tener*, which means "to have" as the verb "to be." It all depends on exactly what you are trying to say. To illustrate this, we will use the phrase, "I am cold," which can mean several different things:

- You may be trying to say that you are a cold person in demeanor and your personality is rather serious or blunt. Since this is a rather permanent trait, you would use the verb *ser* in Spanish, resulting in the phrase "*Yo soy frío.*"
- You may also be trying to say that your body is literally cold since you had a drop in temperature, for whatever reason. This trait is considered to be temporary, in which case you would use *estar* in Spanish, resulting in the phrase "*Yo estoy frío.*"
- Finally, you may be saying that you feel cold and need a sweater. While this trait is also considered to be temporary, it is a trait that you **feel** rather than **have.** Ironically though, you would use the verb *tener* which means "to have" in this scenario, resulting in the phrase "*Yo tengo frío.*"

Like this one there are many other scenarios in which the obvious choice of verb is not always the correct one when conversing with someone in Spanish. However, there are not a lot of instances where this happens, and even if you run into one of said situations it is almost guaranteed that you will still be understood by whoever is talking with you. They will probably correct you though, but there is no reason to feel bad about this. Speaking a new language is a continuous learning experience after all.

Different Dialects Use Different Words

Just like there are different English dialects such as Australian, British, or American English; Spanish also has many different dialects, the two main ones being Spanish from Spain–Castilian Spanish–and Latin American Spanish.

While they share several meanings and uses in their verbs, sometimes a different verb is used to express the same action. An important example of this that you should keep in mind to avoid embarrassing misunderstandings is the verb, "to get." On the list above, we translated it as *'coger.'* That would be the usage in Spain. In Latin America though you should avoid using *'coger'* and say *tomar* instead.

The reason for this is that in Latin America *coger* is more commonly used as a synonym for intercourse. You can see now why there could be some confusion. Not to worry though, most native speakers will be able to tell you don't mean it in a malicious way when you use this verb, there might be some laughs followed by a quick correction.

Besides some uses and meanings, verbs also change some of their conjugations depending on which dialect you are using, but, once again, you will be understood no matter which one you are using. I will point out these differences when we get to them since it is an important step in truly learning Spanish, but for this lesson you don't need to worry.

If you've made it this far then I can tell your dedication is no joke, you are definitely up to the challenge. I got some news for you: you've just finished lesson number one! Give yourself a well-deserved pat on the back. If you feel like it, go back on some of the concepts or verbs you struggled with the most in this chapter, give them one last read and then put down the book.

While you may be eager to continue learning, remember that this challenge was designed to be completed in 5 days and as such you should also be wary of when to stop reading and learning. After all, I relayed a considerable amount of new information to you in this first chapter. Take a break from learning, renew your energy and I will see you tomorrow for the next lesson.

Let's practice

We are all different types of learners. Especially visual, reading and writing learners will benefit from a little practice on paper. Let's see if you have learned the 25 verbs for today and are able to provide the Spanish verb below:

Verb in English	Verb in Spanish
To find	

To drink	
To want	
To have	
To go	
To touch	
To come	
To work	
To bring	
To be (temporarily)	
To need	
To talk	
To do	
To must	
To sleep	
To be able/can	
To go out	
To search	
To be (permanent)	
To put	
To eat	
To give	
To live	
To know	

To get	

Check your answers in the table underneath. Keep repeating the exercise until you feel like you have done it with ease.

Verb in English	Verb in Spanish
To find	Encontrar
To drink	Beber
To want	Querer
To have	Tener
To go	Ir
To touch	Tocar
To come	Venir
To work	Trabajar
To bring	Traer
To be (temporarily)	Estar
To need	Necesitar
To talk	Hablar
To do	Hacer
To must	Deber
To sleep	Dormir
To be able/can	Poder

To go out	Salir
To search	Buscar
To be (permanent)	Ser
To put	Poner
To eat	Comer
To give	Dar
To live	Vivir
To know	Saber
To get	Coger

Day 2: Use the Future Tense With the Help of 6 Little Words

You're back, amazing! Be proud of yourself, most people would've turned their backs after day one. Most of the memorizing is done, so you won't need to worry much about it in today's lesson. In fact, this may be the shortest and easiest lesson of the entire challenge. A good change of pace from yesterday, don't you think?

As the title says, we will be learning how to make the future tense. Logic tells us that you will need to memorize the conjugation of each verb in its future form. This isn't completely true though. While you will need to learn these conjugations eventually, there is a simple way in which you can speak in the future tense without having to memorize all its forms; this is through the use of the verb *ir* in its present tense.

Surely you remember what '*ir*' means, right? Don't worry, you don't need to go back to the verb table if you forgot, I will give you the answer—it means "to go." When you conjugate this verb in present tense throughout the six different subject pronouns you will be able to use the future tense of any verb without changing its infinitive form. Quite a neat shortcut, but how exactly does it work?

First of all, let's see what the six subject pronouns are in Spanish and how the verb *ir* will look for each pronoun:

English pronoun	Spanish pronoun	'Ir' conjugation
I	*Yo*	*Voy*
You	*Tú* (informal), *usted* (formal)	*Vas*
He, She	*Él, Ella*	*Va*
We	*Nosotros*	*Vamos*
You (plural)	*Vosotros (ustedes)*	*Vais (van)*
They	*Ellos, ellas, ustedes*	*Van*

Quick note before we continue, both the pronoun 'vosotros' and the conjugation 'vais' are exclusive to the Spain dialect, and while you will be understood in Latin America if you use these forms, it is uncommon for anyone to speak like that there.

This is all you will have to memorize for today. Way less than yesterday, right? It may help you to know the exact translation of the phrases you are learning though, so here they are:

- *Yo voy* - I go
- *Tú vas* - you go (singular)
- *Él/Ella va* - he/she goes
- *Nosotros vamos* - we go
- *Vosotros vais* - you go (plural)
- *Ellos/Ellas/Ustedes van* - they go

Now that you have memorized these six new words and know exactly what you are saying, it is time I show you a formula that will help you say the future tense of any verb you wish: IR + A + VERB = GO + TO + VERB.

The way this works is by using the verb 'ir' as a phrase that indicates an action will be made at some point in the future. You are literally saying "I'm going to + verb", which also works in the English language to speak in the future tense. The fact that it works in Spanish too raises a huge weight from our shoulders since now we can use any verb, even the ones outside the table of chapter 1, in the future tense. Let's start conjugating the 25 verbs we memorized to make sure you have a good grasp of this trick:

Spanish verb in infinitive	Spanish verb in future	English translation
Ser	Voy a ser	I am going to be
Estar	Vas a estar	You are going to be
Hacer	Vais a hacer	You are going to do
Tener	Van a tener	They are going to have
Ir	Vamos a ir	We are going to go
Hablar	Va a hablar	He/she is going to talk
Coger	Voy a coger	I am going to get
Vivir	Vas a vivir	You are going to live
Traer	Vais a traer	You are going to bring
Beber	Van a beber	They are going to drink

Necesitar	Vamos a necesitar	We are going to need
Tocar	Va a tocar	He/she is going to touch
Querer	Voy a querer	I am going to want
Poner	Vas a poner	You are going to put
Poder	Vais a poder	You are going to be able
Salir	Van a salir	They are going to get out
Buscar	Vamos a buscar	We are going to search
Encontrar	Va a encontrar	He/she is going to find
Dormir	Voy a dormir	I am going to sleep
Saber	Vas a saber	You are going to know
Dar	Vais a dar	You are going to give
Trabajar	Van a trabajar	They are going to work
Comer	Vamos a comer	We are going to eat
Venir	Va a venir	He/she is going to come

As you can see, I didn't put the six different subject pronouns for each verb. If I had, the table would have been too big. This is a great opportunity for you to practice the trick you just learned by conjugating the remaining subjects that are not included in the table without seeing the answers. With the examples I provided above it will be a breeze, especially if you understood the formula.

The future tense we just learned is one of many different future tenses we can use in Spanish. Even if this specific form is used for actions that will take place in the near future or to express an intention, it can be used interchangeably with the future simple tense, making this one of the easiest ways of speaking in the future.

Now that you have the formula down and you were able to conjugate the missing verbs from the table it is time to address some details you may have missed while you were memorizing and practicing this lesson.

Verbs Replacing Subject Pronouns

Pay close attention to the table where I conjugated some of the verbs in Spanish. Notice anything different between the Spanish conjugation and its English counterpart? While the English version maintains its subject pronouns on each conjugation, these are missing in the Spanish translation.

This is not a mistake, it is quite common in the Spanish language to not include the subject pronouns. The verbs will tell us by themselves which subject we are referring to.

However, you won't be wrong if you decide to include the pronoun on each verb you conjugate, it just isn't the way most native speakers talk.

These are the types of small things that separate the good speakers from the great ones, and through constant practice, you will master all these little differences and speak a Spanish that is both grammatically correct and natural.

What About 'Must'?

There is another hidden thing that you most likely missed the first time you read the table with the future conjugations. Count the verbs again: there are only 24. Which one is missing? Well, the title of this segment already gave it away: it is 'must.'

The reason why I didn't include this verb in my conjugations is because this method won't work on every verb. 'Must' is one of these cases in which you will need to use the proper future conjugation in order to correctly make yourself understood.

If you conjugated 'must' with the formula you just learned, the resulting phrase would be, *"Voy a deber,"* which means, "I am going to **owe**," in the everyday way of speaking. If you want to say 'must' in the future tense instead, your best option will be to conjugate the verb rather than rely on the trick you learned in this lesson. There is no reason to worry since conjugating this verb is fairly as it is a regular verb:

- *Yo deberé*
- *Tú deberás*
- *El/Ella deberá*
- *Nosotros deberemos*
- *Vosotros deberéis*
- *Ellos/Ellas/Ustedes deberán*

As you can see, the future conjugation of 'must' is a breeze, you just need to add a few letters to its infinitive form, and you're done! This is possible because, as a regular verb, *'deber'* does not change its stem throughout its different tenses. But what exactly is the stem of a verb?

The answer is part of tomorrow's lesson, we are done for the day. I told you this would be a shorter lesson! How did you feel today? Was this lesson easier or harder than yesterday's? You must be wary of the way you are feeling throughout the day since we want to avoid unnecessary frustrations. If you feel like there are some things you still don't understand completely, now would be a good time to review them. But remember to take some rest and prepare for tomorrow, since we will be tackling the most important lesson of the challenge–the stem of the verbs.

Day 3: How to Form the Stem of the Verb, the Basics of all Conjugations

Prepare yourself, the lesson today will probably be the most useful one when it comes to conjugating verbs. Unfortunately, it may also be the most boring of the whole challenge, so gather all the patience and courage you require and let's dive right in.

Why is it so important to be able to form the stem of the verb? Being able to do so will bring us closer to becoming masters of Spanish conjugation. Think of the stem as the part of a verb from which all its forms and tenses grow, meaning once you identify it, transforming the verb should be an easier task than memorizing each existing form.

In fact, for most of the verbs, all you have to do in order to conjugate them correctly is to identify the stem and add one to four letters to it –then you're done! You've transformed your verb successfully. This is the method for regular verbs, however, there still are the irregular verbs, and even the stem-changing verbs, which are a lot trickier to conjugate correctly. It will take you a lot of practice to be able to learn all the different forms of the verbs, but this doesn't mean you should refrain from speaking Spanish until you have mastered all the verb forms.

Don't worry, I will not ask you to learn all the conjugations for this power challenge. For now, let's focus on the stem and how to find it.

The stem of a regular verbs

If you read the verb list you'll find that all of them end in either -AR, -ER, or -IR. Rule of thumb:

For all regular verb:

> **Form the stem of the verb by removing the last 2 letters (-AR, -IR or -ER)**

That was the easy part. Let's have a look at the regular verbs we have selected in this 5 day challenge. Now you know the rule it should be easy to form the stem:

Spanish verb	Stem	Meaning in English
Hablar	*Habl-*	To talk
Vivir	*Viv-*	To live
Beber	*Beb-*	To drink
Necesitar	*Necesit-*	To need
Deber	*Deb-*	To must
Trabajar	*Trabaj-*	To work
Comer	*Com-*	To eat

| Tocar | Toc- | To touch |
| Buscar | Busc- | To search |

There should be little to no problems for you when identifying the stem of these verbs since they follow the set formula: just remove the last two letters! On to the next set of verbs.

About half of all Spanish verbs are regular, which means that with this simple rule, you know how to create the stem of about half of all Spanish verbs. In the next chapter you will learn how to conjugate them.

The stem of a irregular verbs

Not all Spanish verbs are regular and there are different verbs that have their own set of rules. When we say a verb is irregular in Spanish, we simply mean the stem changes and does not always comply with the rule above. It is something you simply have to know.

To make it easy for you, there are 4 different kinds of irregular verbs. Let's categorize them and see what we are dealing with:

Vowel changes in yo, tú, el and ellos form.	Only yo/I changes	Combination of column A and B	Completely irregular
Querer	*Hacer*	*Venir*	Ser
Poder	*Coger*	*Tener*	Estar
Encontrar	*Traer*		Ir
Dormir	*Poner*		
	Salir		
	Saber		
	Dar		

Vowel changes in yo, tú, el and ellos form.

It is quite common for Spanish verbs to change stem, however only in the persona Yo, Tú, Él, Ella, Ellos, Ellas and Ustedes. When we deal with an irregular stem changing verbs than a vowel will change into the following:

E > IE or E > I

O > UE

U > UE

Let's make a table underneath and see how the stem changes. Let's mark the columns that behave irregular with a light grey background.

Vowel changes in yo, tu, el and ellos form.	Yo	Tú	Él, Ella, Usted	Nosotros	Vosotros	Ellos, Ellas, Ustedes
Querer	*quier*	*quier*	*quier*	quer	quer	*quier*
Poder	*pued*	*pued*	*pued*	pod	pod	*pued*
Encontrar	*encuentr*	*encuentr*	*encuentr*	encontr	encontr	*encuentr*
Dormir	*duerm*	*duerm*	*duerm*	dorm	dorm	*duerm*

Only yo (I) changes

There are quite a few irregular Spanish verbs where only "I" changes. These are verbs that change stems and don't follow the formula that regular verbs do. However, the stem changes in these verbs are not as radical as other stem-changing verbs, you only need to replace one letter with another or add an extra letter. All other 5 stems are formed according to the regular rule where you only take off the last few letters.

Let's look at the stem of the following verbs where we can see only the first form changes stem:

Spanish verb.	Yo	Tú	Él, Ella, Usted	Nosotros	Vosotros	Ellos, Ellas, Ustedes
Hacer	Hag	Hac	Hac	Hac	Hac	Hac
Coger	Coj	Cog	Cog	Cog	Cog	Cog
Traer	Traig	Trae	Trae	Trae	Trae	Trae
Poner	Pong	Pon	Pon	Pon	Pon	Pon
Salir	Salg	Sal	Sal	Sal	Sal	Sal
Saber	*	Sab	Sab	Sab	Sab	Sab
Dar	*	D	D	D	D	D

* indicates this form is completely irregular, which we will go into in the next chapter.

Stems that change the first form and vowels

This category has two verbs: Venir and Tener. You will see that the the rules of the first two forms of irregular forms apply to these verbs. Let's have a look at how the stem behaves in these cases. The irregular columns have a grey background.

Spanish verb.	Yo	Tú	Él, Ella, Usted	Nosotros	Vosotros	Ellos, Ellas, Ustedes
Tener	*Teng*	*Tien*	*Tien*	*Ten*	*Ten*	*Tien*
Venir	*Veng*	*Tien*	*Tien*	*Ven*	*Ven*	*Tien*

You can see how we won't add the same letter to all the subjects, while others don't add an extra letter at all. These are specific cases which you will have to memorize, but with practice you will master it in no time.

Completely irregular verbs

When we try to conjugate all the verbs we'll run into some trouble and confusion along the way. Because of this, I'll go along with the list explaining some interesting cases and how to get their stem.

First is the verb '*ser.*' If we remove -ER we are only left with an 's'. Is this really the stem of the verb? Not particularly. '*Ser*' is what we would consider a verb with a changing stem, meaning it will have different stems for different subjects. For example, in the present tense it will both have "So" and "E" as stems, resulting in the following conjugations:

- *Yo **soy***
- *Tú **eres***
- *Él/Ella **es***
- *Nosotros **so**mos*
- *Vosotros **so**is/ Ustedes **son***
- *Ellos/ Ellas **son***

These types of verbs tend to have different stems between tenses too, adding up to four– or even more–stems for one verb. They are the hardest verbs to master because of this.

The next verbs in our list are *'estar'* and *'ir'*, which are all irregular. Remember that an irregular verb changes its stem when conjugated and/or it doesn't follow the usual formula for conjugation that regular verbs follow.

Regarding *'estar,'* this is a verb whose stem won't change but it doesn't follow the regular verbs' conjugation formula. This means that finding its stem is easy, but the conjugation will require some more work. We won't get into great detail about this since those are problems for the next chapters. Right now, we are looking for the stems, how would it look in this verb? After we remove the -ER we are left with 'est.' This will be the stem for all the subjects and all the tenses, making *'estar'* one of the easiest irregular verbs to conjugate:

- *Yo **est**oy*
- *Tú **est**ás*
- *Él/Ella **est**á*
- *Nosotros **est**amos*
- *Vosotros **est**áis/ Ustedes **est**án*
- *Ellos **est**án*

Up next, we have perhaps one of the hardest verbs to conjugate in Spanish: *'ir'*. As you can see, we can't go with our usual method of removing the -IR termination to find the stem since then we would be left with no verb at all! That means we will have to memorize the different stems it has in the different tenses.

- 'va-' for the present tense
- 'fu-' for the past tense
- 'ir-' for the future tense

Fortunately, we have already seen *'ir'* conjugation in the present tense in yesterday's lesson, so that is one less verb to the list. However, I have added it below as a recap so it is fresh in your memory:

- *Yo **voy***
- *Tú **vas***
- *Él/ Ella **va***
- *Nosotros **vamos***
- *Vosotros **váis**/ ustedes **van***
- *Ellos **van***

While it is confusing to understand why a verb would change so much, situations like this are scarce. Not many verbs go through this many modifications and the ones who do tend to be the first ones you learn–getting the hardest part out of the way.

With the past examples, you should have a general idea of the different situations you will encounter when obtaining the stem of any verb. For now, I will make the job easier by dividing our 25 verbs into regular verbs, irregular non-changing stem verbs, and irregular changing stem verbs, as well as pointing out each of their stems. Starting with the easier ones–the regular verbs.

Overview of all stems in the present tense

We saw at the beginning of this chapter that some verbs have different stems depending on the tense we are using. While you will, eventually, have to face these stem changes, if you plan to continue learning Spanish, for now, we will just focus on the stem of the present tense since this will be the topic for tomorrow.

Find a full overview in the table underneath of the stems:

Spanish verb	Present tense stem	Meaning in English
Hablar	*Habl-*	To talk
Vivir	*Viv-*	To live
Beber	*Beb-*	To drink
Necesitar	*Necesit-*	To need
Deber	*Deb-*	To must
Trabajar	*Trabaj-*	To work
Comer	*Com-*	To eat
Tocar	*Toc-*	To touch
Buscar	*Busc-*	To search
Ser	*So-/E-*	To be (permanent)

Estar	Est-	To be (temporary)
Hacer	Hag-/Hac-	To do
Tener	Ten-/Tien-	To have
Ir	Vo-/Va-	To go
Coger	Coj-/Cog-	To take
Tocar	Toc-	To touch
Querer	Quier-/Quer-	To want
Poner	Pon-	To put
Poder	Pued-/Pod-	To be able/can
Buscar	Busc-	To search
Encontrar	Encuentr-/Encontr-	To find
Dormir	Duerm-/Dorm	To sleep
Saber	Se/Sab-	To know
Dar	Do-/Da-	To give
Venir	Ven-/Vien-	To come

Practice makes perfect

Let's see how well you are able to master today's information. We are going to put it to the test. Fill in the "Present tense stem" column underneath and check your answers in the table above.

Spanish verb	Present tense stem	Meaning in English
Hablar		To talk
Vivir		To live
Beber		To drink
Necesitar		To need
Deber		To must
Trabajar		To work
Comer		To eat
Tocar		To touch
Buscar		To search
Ser		To be (permanent)
Estar		To be (temporary)
Hacer		To do
Tener		To have
Ir		To go
Coger		To take
Tocar		To touch
Querer		To want
Poner		To put
Poder		To be able/can
Buscar		To search

Encontrar		To find
Dormir		To sleep
Saber		To know
Dar		To give
Venir		To come

Why Do Stems Change so Much?

Ah, the million-dollar question. You must be wondering why a verb would need up to four different stems to conjugate it. Wouldn't it be easier to just have one? Or that all verbs followed the regular verb formula? Certainly. However, this is not the case in most languages, including English. Regarding the Spanish language, most of the time these are just conventions that were decided when Spanish was just starting to be 'created' so to speak. Of course, there have been significant modifications between today's Spanish and the Spanish spoken centuries ago, but most of the conventions still stand.

You will find that some stem changes do follow some reasoning, mostly based on the correct pronunciation of a word. For the purposes of this book, we won't delve too deeply into these rules since there are too many and our main focus right now is for you to be able to speak Spanish easily as a kickstart to your studies. However, In the future, when you are learning about pronunciation rules and cases, you will see why some verbs need to change their stem.

That's about it for this chapter! I know all the information I just relayed to you may seem overwhelming, but I promise you it will be easier to assimilate once you start putting into practice the concepts you just learned, via exercises and real conversations. Besides, you don't need to memorize all the information you just read. Remember that the majority of the verbs in the Spanish language are regular, which means they follow the same conjugation formula. Several of the most used verbs just happen to be irregular, but look on the bright side! After finishing this challenge, you will have tackled some of the hardest verbs!

We are past the midway point–Keep up the good pace. I can assure you the hardest parts are behind us now. It would be unfortunate to leave it here, so rest your eyes and your brain and make sure to come back tomorrow for our next lesson: the present tense.

Day 4: Time to Learn the Present Tense. Simple!

Compared to yesterday's lesson, this one should be a walk in the park! I know there was a lot of information you had to review, but it was important for you to master this next lesson in no time: conjugating in the present tense.

While we have a trick for the past and the future tense, when it comes to the present tense the only way is through. Not to worry though! If you've mastered, or at least have a general idea of, the stems we reviewed in the past lesson there won't be many problems. The present has the easiest conjugations since it has the least amount of stem changes and almost every verb, regular or irregular, follows the same steps.

First of all, see what the termination of the verb you are about to conjugate is. Is it -AR, -ER, or -IR? The table below will tell you which path to follow since there are different rules for each termination:

Person	-AR verbs	-ER verbs	-IR verbs
Yo	stem + o	stem + o	stem + o
Tú/usted	stem + as	stem + es	stem + es
Él/ella	stem + a	stem + e	stem + e
Nosotros	stem + amos	stem + emos	stem + imos
Vosotros (ustedes)	stem + áis/an	stem + éis/en	stem + ís/en
Ellos/ellas/ustedes	stem + an	stem + en	stem + en

You will note that the verbs may have two different ways of writing them in the second person plural (*vosotros, ustedes*). This is, again, a difference between Castilian Spanish–from Spain–and Latin American Spanish: The first form (*vosotros*) is used in the Spain dialect while the second (*ustedes*) is the norm in the Latin American dialect.

If you follow this simple table, you will be able to conjugate 9 of the 25 verbs in the list already. Why don't you try to do this before continuing? I have already written these verbs in the next table, so, all you have to do is focus on conjugating the verbs correctly. Be sure to remember which steps you must take for every specific termination.

Verb	Yo	Tú	Él / Ella	Nosotros	Vosotros/ Ustedes	Ellos/ Ellas
Hablar						
Vivir						
Beber						
Necesitar						
Deber						
Trabajar						
Comer						
Tocar						
Buscar						

Those who have an observant eye probably noticed that most of the verbs in this table are regular verbs. That is why it is so easy to conjugate them! How many do you think you got right? Check the answers below to find out.

Verb	Yo	Tú	Él / Ella	Nosotros	Vosotros/ Ustedes	Ellos/ Ellas
Hablar	*Hablo*	*Hablas*	*Habla*	*Hablamos*	*Habláis/ Hablan*	*Hablan*
Vivir	*Vivo*	*Vives*	*Vive*	*Vivimos*	*Vivís/ Viven*	*Viven*
Beber	*Bebo*	*Bebes*	*Bebe*	*Bebemos*	*Bebeís/ Beben*	*Beben*
Necesitar	*Necesito*	*Necesitas*	*Necesita*	*Necesitamos*	*Necesitáis/ Necesitan*	*Necesitan*
Deber	*Debo*	*Debes*	*Debe*	*Debemos*	*Debeís/ Deben*	*Deben*
Trabajar	*Trabajo*	*Trabajas*	*Trabaja*	*Trabajamos*	*Trabajáis/ Trabajan*	*Trabajan*
Comer	*Como*	*Comes*	*Come*	*Comemos*	*Coméis/ Comen*	*Comen*
Tocar	*Toco*	*Tocas*	*Toca*	*Tocamos*	*Tocáis/ Tocan*	*Tocan*
Buscar	*Busco*	*Buscas*	*Busca*	*Buscamos*	*Buscáis/ Buscan*	*Buscan*

Did you do alright? Be sure to repeat the exercise and revise the mistakes you made before continuing. I'm sure with two more tries you'll get a perfect score! Before we take a small break, try to conjugate the next set of verbs.

Some verbs, that have two different stems, actually use one stem exclusively for the first person singular (I/ *Yo*), while all the other subjects share the remaining stem. What's more, conjugating the verb in the first person singular follows the steps detailed in the first table of the chapter: you will need to add an 'o' after the stem plus one or two extra letters in order to have the correct pronunciation.

For this next exercise I will give you the correct conjugation of the verbs in the first person singular (*yo*), you will only have to fill in the remaining subjects following the steps you've already practiced. Be sure to memorize the first column of conjugations for the next exercises.

Verb	Yo	Tú	Él/Ella	Nosotros	Vosotros/Ustedes	Ellos/Ellas
Estar	Estoy					
Traer	Traigo					
Salir	Salgo					
Hacer	Hago					
Ir	Voy					
Poner	Pongo					
Coger	Cojo					
Dar	Doy					
Venir	Vengo					

Feeling confident? If you've managed to conjugate the verbs correctly that means you have 18 of the 25 verbs down. That's huge! You are making some really good progress. Before continuing to the next verbs though, let's see if you got all of the forms from the previous exercise right:

Verb	Yo	Tú	Él / Ella	Nosotros	Vosotros/ Ustedes	Ellos/ Ellas
Estar	Estoy	Estás	Está	Estamos	Estáis/ Están	Están
Traer	Traigo	Traes	Trae	Traemos	Traéis/ Traen	Traen
Salir	Salgo	Sales	Sale	Salimos	Salís/ Salen	Salen
Hacer	Hago	Haces	Hace	Hacemos	Hacéis/ Hacen	Hacen
Ir	Voy	Vas	Va	Vamos	Váis/ Van	Van
Poner	Pongo	Pones	Pone	Ponemos	Ponéis/ Ponen	Ponen
Coger	Cojo	Coges	Coge	Cogemos	Cogéis/ Cogen	Cogen
Dar	Doy	Das	Da	Damos	Dáis/ Dan	Dan
Venir	Vengo	Vas	Va	Vamos	Váis/ Van	Van

If you've learned and followed the formula from the beginning of the chapter, I'm sure you had no problems with this exercise. If you are still feeling a little doubtful though, make sure to review and do the exercise again if necessary. It would be optimal that you master these conjugations before continuing. However, you can always take a break before practicing again, or move to other themes if you feel frustrated with this particular lesson but still have some energy to keep studying. Once you clear your mind a little, you'll find that the exercises are easier.

Next up, we have verbs that have a different stem *only* for the first person plural (we/ *nosotros*). Like in the past table, I will provide the correct conjugation for distinct stems and you will have to fill in the rest of the table. Make sure to memorize the conjugations I provide to you already as best as you can:

Verb	Yo	Tú	Él / Ella	Nosotros	Vosotros/ Ustedes	Ellos/ Ellas
Querer				Queremos		
Poder				Podemos		
Encontrar				Encontramos		
Dormir				Dormimos		

A short exercise, right? But are you sure you identified and used the correct stem for the conjugations? If we go back to the table in the past chapter with the stem-changing verbs we will notice that these four verbs change their stems by adding letters. Did you remember this while you were solving the exercise? Don't worry if you didn't, that's why we are practicing in the first place. Below you can check the correct conjugations of these verbs:

Verb	Yo	Tú	Él / Ella	Nosotros	Vosotros/ Ustedes	Ellos/ Ellas
Querer	Quiero	Quieres	Quiere	Queremos	Queréis/ Quieren	Quieren
Poder	Puedo	Puedes	Puede	Podemos	Podéis/ Pueden	Pueden
Encontrar	Encuentro	Encuentras	Encuentra	Encontramos	Encontráis/ Encuentran	Encuentran
Dormir	Duermo	Duermes	Duerme	Dormimos	Dormís/ Duermen	Duermen

Thanks to their changes in the stem, these are some tricky verbs. Fortunately, there aren't a lot of verbs in our list that have stem changes, so memorizing them shouldn't be complicated for you. Now that you've checked your answers, try solving the exercise again to see if you have learned how the stem changes in these four verbs.

Finally, we have reached the last three verbs. I left them until the end because they have some interesting traits when we conjugate them, so it's best if we study them separately in order to give them our full attention. Take your time in these last conjugations and make sure you have a good idea of how they work before moving to the next one.

Conjugating 'Ser'

The verb 'ser,' which is the equivalent to the verb "to be," is one of the verbs that changes the most when conjugated. If you think about it, that is also the case in the English language: we have 'am', 'are', and 'is' as different conjugations in the present tense. For this verb, you will have to memorize its conjugation since the rules we learned in the beginning won't apply. Having said this, they are:

- *Yo soy*
- *Tú eres*
- *Él/Ella es*
- *Nosotros somos*
- *Vosotros sóis/ustedes son*
- *Ellos/Ellas son*

You may have noticed that this conjugation was already shown in yesterday's lesson. However, since today we are learning about the present tense conjugation it is important and relevant to see this verb once again. As such, you should review these conjugations as much as you need to. It doesn't matter if you take more time to get it right, after all, this is one of the verbs you will use the most when speaking Spanish, mastering it is a necessity.

Conjugating '*Tener*'

Remember how some verbs will have a different stem for the first person of the singular while others differ in the first person of the plural? Well, when it comes to the verb '*tener*', which means 'to have', both first persons share the "ten-" stem, while the rest of the subjects share the "tien-" stem. Here is what the conjugation would look like:

- *Yo tengo*
- *Tú tienes*
- *Él/Ella tiene*
- *Nosotros tenemos*
- *Vosotros tenéis/ustedes tienen*
- *Ellos/Ellas tienen*

Even though this verb has two stems, you can see how the method we have been following for most of the exercises still works. However, it is time we address the difference between '*vosotros*' and '*ustedes*' and how this can affect both the stem and the conjugation of the verbs.

Vosotros vs Ustedes

In lesson two I mentioned how '*vosotros*' is a pronoun primarily used in Spain while '*ustedes*' is the common form in Latin America. This resulted in the verbs having two possible conjugations for one person in the present tense. You most likely noticed how there was a column that always had two verb conjugations instead of one, this is why.

However, having two different ways for referring to the same person can also change the stem of some verbs in the same conjugation. This can be seen in the answers to the last table you filled. While this guide includes both conjugations in order to teach you both dialects, it is best that you focus on one of the dialects to avoid extra confusion and then come back to the other one, if you want to. Rest assured that no matter which Spanish 'version' you choose, you will be understood by any Spanish speaker.

If you are eager to learn both versions though, a useful trick is to remember that the verb conjugation for *"ustedes"* will always be the same as the conjugation for *"ellos/ ellas."* This makes the Latin American conjugation slightly easier, but it also means that if you focus on the Spain dialect you will inadvertently learn all you need for the Latin American dialect. It's a win-win situation!

Conjugating '*Saber*'

Finally we have the verb '*saber*' which means "to know". This verb has a different stem for the first person singular while the rest of the subjects share another stem. We had a table with verbs like these earlier so why did I separate this verb specifically?

In that table, even if the first person singular changed the stem, the steps you follow to conjugate are similar, since you will add the letter 'o' to the stem plus some extra letters. However, in the verb '*saber*' the letter 'o' won't be found anywhere, instead we use an 'e' with an accent:

- *Yo sé*
- *Tú sabes*
- *Él/Ella sabe*
- *Nosotros sabemos*
- *Vosotros sabéis/ Ustedes saben*
- *Ellos/Ellas saben*

This is the only instance in our 25 verbs where a conjugation doesn't follow the method we learned at all. Maybe this exception will make it stick out to you and it will be easier to learn, but it is okay if you find it hard to remember when you are engaging in a conversation. Repetition and constant practice through speaking and doing exercises will make you learn all these verbs little by little.

One Last Review

Speaking of repetition, how about we practice with some final exercises to review what we saw in this lesson? I will be putting a simple English phrase using the present tense and you will try to translate it to Spanish. It's okay if you can't translate it without help at first, you can go and reread past sections of this chapter, but do try to translate on your own where you can. Ready? Here we go:

Verb in English	Spanish Translation
They are	
I make	

We talk	
You go out (singular)	
She sleeps	
You work (plural)	
We bring	
They must	
He puts	
I want	
We touch	
You need (plural)	
They know	
She gives	
You live (singular)	

And done! You have completed the last exercise of this chapter, extraordinary work! If you were able to apply all you learned today, this last exercise mustn't have been a challenge for you. Want to see how well you did? Here are the answers:

Verb in English	Spanish Translation
They are	*Ellos son*
I make	*Yo hago*

We talk	*Nosotros hablamos*
You go out (singular)	*Tú sales*
She sleeps	*Ella duerme*
You work (plural)	*Vosotros trabajáis/ ustedes trabajan*
We bring	*Nosotros traemos*
They must	*Ellos/ Ellas deben*
He puts	*Él pone*
I want	*Yo quiero*
We touch	*Nosotros tocamos*
You need (plural)	*Vosotros necesitáis/ Ustedes necesitan*
They know	*Ellos/ Ellas saben*
She gives	*Ella da*
You live (singular)	*Tú vives*

I know there was a lot of practice during this chapter, but you must start testing your knowledge and identifying which areas you may be failing in. It's all part of the process. The good news is, we are done for today! How does it feel to be so close to the finish line? Your dedication and hard work have taken you far, I'm proud of you. I hope you come back tomorrow, for the last day of the challenge!

Day 5: A Simple Trick to Form the Past Tense

Welcome to the last day of the challenge! Are you feeling relieved that it's almost over? Sad that the week went by so fast? Hungry for more? No matter what though, it was your effort that brought you this far and you should be proud of that. So, are you ready to tackle the last lesson? Let's get down to business.

Today we will be dealing with the past tense in Spanish. Bear in mind that the Spanish language has several different past tenses. For this lesson, though, you will only be learning one. This will allow you to avoid memorizing even more conjugations. Be aware that you will have to learn them eventually but, thanks to the trick you will learn today, you will be understood when speaking Spanish, even if another past tense was more appropriate for the situation you were in.

This past tense is formed by the verb *'haber'* using a specific conjugation, plus any verb in its past participle form. Firstly, here's how to conjugate the verb *'haber.'*

Conjugation in Spanish	Meaning in english
He	I have
Has	You have (singular)
Ha	He/She has

Hemos	We have
Habéis/Han	You have (plural)
Han	They have

This conjugation will be the cornerstone for using this trick so make sure you know it by heart. How does the trick work? It all relies on the meaning of the verb '*haber.*'

'*Haber*' in Spanish means "to have." This may confuse you since the verb '*tener*' also means "to have." The difference here is that '*tener*' refers to possessing things: I have blond hair, I have a ball, I have a backpack. On the other hand, '*haber*' in this context is the kind of "to have" that refers to what you have been doing: I have been driving, I have been sleeping, I have been working.

Now that we know exactly what we are saying, it's time to conjugate the verbs in their participle form. For most of them it won't be too hard since they follow the same formula—even if they are irregular verbs. The formula is:

- STEM + ado for the verbs ending in -AR
- STEM + ido for the verbs ending in -ER
- STEM + ido for the verbs ending in -ER

Below I have written all the conjugations in participle or '*participio*' for our 25 verbs. You will see that almost all of them follow the formula, but there are some exceptions so pay close attention to the table and try to identify them:

Spanish Verb	Participio (*Participio*)	English Translation
Ser	*Sido*	Been (permanent)
Estar	*Estado*	Been (temporary)
Hacer	*Hecho* *	Done
Tener	*Tenido*	Had
Ir	*Ido*	Gone
Hablar	*Hablado*	Talked
Coger	*Cogido*	Got
Vivir	*Vivido*	Lived
Traer	*Traído*	Brought
Beber	*Bebido*	Drunk
Necesitar	*Necesitado*	Needed
Tocar	*Tocado*	Touched
Querer	*Querido*	Wanted
Comprar	*Comprado*	Bought
Poner	*Puesto* *	Put
Poder	*Podido*	Been able to
Salir	*Salido*	Gone out
Buscar	*Buscado*	Searched
Encontrar	*Encontrado*	Found
Dormir	*Dormido*	Slept

Saber	*Sabido*	Known
Dar	*Dado*	Given
Trabajar	*Trabajado*	Worked
Comer	*Comido*	Eaten
Venir	*Venido*	Came

*Please note all conjugations are according to the rules above with the exception of two: Hacer and Poner. They live by their own rules and have an irregular participle.

Why did I decide to show you this past tense instead of the past simple? If I had shown you the past simple you would have learned six different conjugations, one for each person, for each verb. That's too many! This way you are only learning one conjugation per verb, plus the six we saw at the beginning. It is a much simpler method which has pretty much the same meaning as the simple past tense when speaking in Spanish.

Learning the participle might seem a little uncomfortable at first but, with constant practice, you will be able to convert verbs into their participle form with ease. That's the key to this whole challenge: *practice*. You can only learn a new language if you keep practicing and studying it and, while it may help to learn some tips and tricks to make it easier, in the end it depends on your resolve.

Having said this–it is time to celebrate! This is the end of today's lesson, which means you have finished the *5 Day Spanish Verb Power Challenge*, congratulations! In less than a week you have learned what most people take months, or even years, to master. However, this knowledge will only be maintained if you keep practicing what you've learned today. That means, it is almost time to go out there and start talking using all you learned. But before that, you will have to face some final exercises to make sure you master *all* the lessons.

Let's practice

Practice makes perfect. Let's see if you can translate the following sentences:

English	Translate to Spanish
I have eaten	
We have slept	
They have bought	
You (plural) have talked	
He has found	
She has had	
You (singular) have lived	
I have drunk	
We have worked	
You (plural) have searched	
I have wanted	
He has gone out	

They have put	
You (singular) have known	
They have gotten	
She has done	
I have given	
He has touched	
We have gone	
I have found	
I have slept	
You have given	
They have drunk	
You (plural) have bought	

Check if your answers are correct in the table underneath:

English	**Translate to Spanish**
I have eaten	He comido
We have slept	Hemos dormido
They have bought	Han traído
You (plural) have talked	Habéis/Han hablado
He has found	Ha encontrado
She has had	Ha tenido

You (singular) have lived	Has vivido
I have drunk	He bebido
We have worked	Hemos trabajado
You (plural) have searched	Habéis/Han buscado
I have wanted	He querido
He has gone out	Ha salido
They have put	Han puesto
You (singular) have known	Has sabido
They have gotten	Han cogido
She has done	Ha hecho
I have given	He dado
He has touched	Ha tocado
We have gone	Hemos ido
I have found	He encontrado
I have slept	He dormido
You have given	Has dado
They have drunk	Han bebido
You (plural) have bought	Habéis/Han traído

Final Exercises

We are here, the goal is within reach. I'll admit these have been five long days filled with lots of information; But, you never gave up. So, before you go and show the world what you've learned, let's have one last review to test your knowledge. I hope you're up to the task.

For this last test, you will have to translate groups of three phrases into their Spanish counterparts. As usual, the answers will be at the end of the exercises. Don't cheat!

Verbs	Spanish Translation
I work	
I am going to work	
I have worked	
You eat (singular)	
You are going to eat (singular)	
You have eaten (singular)	
He is	
He is going to be	
He has been	
She touches	
She is going to touch	

She has touched	
We know	
We are going to know	
We have known	
You sleep (plural)	
You are going to sleep (plural)	
You have slept (plural)	
They go out	
They are going to go out	
They have gone out	
She lives	
She is going to live	
She has lived	
We talk	
We are going to talk	
We have talked	
You get (plural)	
You are going to get (plural)	
You have got (plural)	
He gives	
He is going to give	
He has given	

I want	
I am going to want	
I have wanted	
They need	
They are going to need	
They have needed	
You drink (singular)	
You are going to drink (singular)	
You have drunk (singular)	
He brings	
They are going to bring	
I have brought	
We search	
You are going to search (plural)	
You have searched (singular)	
You go (plural)	
She is going to go	
I have gone	

How was that? Did it feel complicated or was it child's play? Anxious to see your answers? Well, I don't want to keep you waiting, check for yourself to see how well you did!

Verbs	Spanish Translation
I work	*Yo trabajo*
I am going to work	*Yo voy a trabajar*
I have worked	*Yo he trabajado*
You eat (singular)	*Tú comes*
You are going to eat (singular)	*Tú vas a comer*
You have eaten (singular)	*Tú has comido*
He is	*Él es or Él está*
He is going to be	*Él va a ser/ Él va a estar*
He has been	*Él ha sido/ Él ha estado*
She touches	*Ella toca*
She is going to touch	*Ella va a tocar*
She has touched	*Ella ha tocado*
We know	*Nosotros sabemos*
We are going to know	*Nosotros vamos a saber*
We have known	*Nosotros hemos sabido*
You sleep (plural)	*Vosotros dormís/ Ustedes duermen*
You are going to sleep (plural)	*Vosotros váis a dormir/ Ustedes van a dormir*
You have slept (plural)	*Vosotros habéis dormido/ Ustedes han dormido*
They go out	*Ellos/Ellas salen*
They are going to go out	*Ellos/Ellas van a salir*

They have gone out	Ellos/Ellas han salido
She lives	Ella vive
She is going to live	Ella va a vivir
She has lived	Ella ha vivido
We talk	Nosotros hablamos
We are going to talk	Nosotros vamos a hablar
We have talked	Nosotros hemos hablado
You get (plural)	Vosotros cogéis/ Ustedes cogen
You are going to get (plural)	Vosotros váis a coger/ Ustedes van a coger
You have got (plural)	Vosotros habéis cogido / Ustedes han cogido
He gives	Él da
He is going to give	Él va a dar
He has given	Él ha dado
I want	Yo quiero
I am going to want	Yo voy a querer
I have wanted	Yo he querido
They need	Ellos/ Ellas necesitan
They are going to need	Ellos/Ellas van a necesitar
They have needed	Ellos/ Ellas han necesitado
You drink (singular)	Tú bebes
You are going to drink (singular)	Tú vas a beber

You have drunk (singular)	*Tú has bebido*
He brings	*Él trae*
They are going to bring	*Ellos/Ellas van a traer*
I have brought	*Yo he traído*
We search	*Nosotros buscamos*
You are going to search (plural)	*Vosotros váis a buscar/ Ustedes van a buscar*
You have searched (singular)	*Tú has buscado*
You go (plural)	*Vosotros váis/ Ustedes van*
She is going to go	*Ella vas a ir*
I have gone	*Yo he ido*

It's okay if you didn't get them all correct on the first try since you needed to use everything you learned during the last five days. It was made to indicate what areas you need to improve and which ones you've already mastered. Don't be afraid to go back and look over the material if your first try wasn't successful. You've gotten this far, so revising one last time won't be hard. You've already powered through five days of memorizing and learning after all!

Conclusion: Where to Go Next?

So you've made it to the end of the book. If you understood the lessons, you should now be prepared to have simple conversations in Spanish. Sure, you may commit some mistakes, but that's just a natural part of the process! Besides, no one will berate you if you forget something or use a tense wrong, so you shouldn't either. Bear in mind that Spanish is a difficult language, native speakers have been 'practicing' it since they were born and most of them don't really know how it works either.

Now, it's time to put your abilities to the test. The best way to continue practicing is by speaking Spanish with other people, even if it's at a simple level. Try to listen to real conversations as well in order to train your ear. You may be able to speak it, but can you understand it? Remember that one half of having conversations is listening to the other person.

Maybe it will be difficult for some to start speaking Spanish, not because they don't want to or are afraid to put their skills to the test, but because they don't know anyone who is learning the language. Not to worry though, thanks to the Internet you can connect with people who are also learning and practice together. Maybe they can recommend their own methods and tricks and you can do the same! Knowledge is meant to be shared and it grows faster with company.

The most important tip I can give you for the future is to keep yourself motivated. Find a meaningful reason to continue learning and practicing Spanish: it could be to connect with more people, travel around the world, or even impress those around you. Any reason is valid as long as it serves as your fuel.

As for this book, it is important to remember that I made this challenge to kickstart your Spanish journey and help you speak as soon as possible. You can always come back to this challenge if you feel lost or like there is something you still struggle with. However, if you want to keep going and have more complex conversations then you should definitely do that. So, what should be the next thing you learn?

I personally recommend you slowly start expanding your vocabulary in the nouns department. After all, verbs are only one half of a phrase, you are still missing the 'subjects.' A good exercise is to go about your day paying attention to what things you use and the actions you do. Certainly, you will find yourself doing one of the verbs in this book, but you will struggle to describe, in full, what you are doing since the noun is still missing. Make a list of these things you do every day and start looking for their Spanish translations.

Another set of words you should start learning are prepositions. They are easy to memorize but hard to master; The sooner you can incorporate them into your Spanish, the better off you'll be since they will help you a great deal when speaking. You will be understood more easily and it will allow for a higher level of specificity.

Also, keep in mind that you will have to learn some pronunciation and grammatical rules. Delving into them with this previous knowledge will make the task much easier though, and you will understand the reason behind some of the conjugations and changes presented in this book.

Finally, don't disregard this book now that you have started your Spanish journey. Even though this guide was written for beginners, the lessons presented here will be useful at any level of expertise. Make sure to come back from time to time, if not to learn a new thing at least to verify how far you've grown since your first contact with the Spanish language.

Thank you for taking up this challenge, I'm happy that you saw it through to the end! I hope this challenge comes in handy again, at some other point in the future. By then, I'm sure you won't be a beginner anymore.

BONUS: Spanish conjugation blueprint

Since you have learned the stem of the verbs in this *5 day - Spanish verb power challenge* you are one step away of conjugating in all Spanish tenses. However, learning 24 different in tenses is something that simply sounds impossible

Spanish Regular Verb
conjugation blueprint

-AR Verbs

Present	Past	Future	Potential Simple
Hablo – I talk	Hablé – I talked	Hablaré – I'll talk	Hablaría – I'd speak
yo stem + o	yo stem + é	yo stem + aré	yo stem + aría
tú stem + as	tú stem + aste	tú stem + arás	tú stem + arías
él stem + a	él stem + ó	él stem + ará	él stem + aría
nosotros stem + amos	nosotros stem + amos	nosotros stem + aremos	nosotros stem + aríamos
vosotros stem + áis	vosotros stem + asteis	vosotros stem + aréis	vosotros stem + aríais
ellos stem + an	ellos stem + aron	ellos stem + arán	ellos stem + arían

-ER Verbs

Present	Past	Future	Potential Simple
Como – I eat	Comí – I ate	Comeré – I'll eat	Comería – I'd eat
yo stem + o	yo stem + í	yo stem + eré	yo stem + ería
tú stem + es	tú stem + iste	tú stem + erás	tú stem + erías
él stem + e	él stem + ió	él stem + erá	él stem + ería
nosotros stem + emos	nosotros stem + imos	nosotros stem + eremos	nosotros stem + eríamos
vosotros stem + éis	vosotros stem + isteis	vosotros stem + eréis	vosotros stem + eríais
ellos stem + en	ellos stem + ieron	ellos stem + erán	ellos stem + erían

-IR Verbs

Present	Past	Future	Potential Simple
Vivo – I live	Viví – I lived	Viviré – I'll live	Viviría – I'd live
yo stem + o	yo stem + í	yo stem + iré	yo stem + iría
tú stem + es	tú stem + iste	tú stem + irás	tú stem + irías
él stem + e	él stem + ió	él stem + irá	él stem + iría
nosotros stem + imos	nosotros stem + imos	nosotros stem + iremos	nosotros stem + iríamos
vosotros stem + ís	vosotros stem + isteis	vosotros stem + iréis	vosotros stem + iríais
ellos stem + en	ellos stem + ieron	ellos stem + irán	ellos stem + irían

Participle
-AR verbs = stem + ado
-IR verbs = stem + ido
-ER verbs = stem + ido

Perfect Indicative
He caminado
I have walked
he participle
has participle
ha participle
hemos participle
habéis participle
han participle

Past Perfect Subjunctive
Hubiera caminado
I would have walked
hubiera participle
hubieras participle
hubiera participle
hubiéramos participle
hubierais participle
hubieran participle

Gerund
-AR verb = stem + ando
-ER and -IR verb = stem + iendo

Present Continous
Estoy caminando
I am walking
yo estoy gerund
tú estás gerund
él está gerund
nosotros estamos gerund
vosotros estáis gerund
ellos están gerund

There are over 360 regular verbs in Spanish.
Start practicing with these:

Regular -AR verb
Aceptar (accept), Crear (create), Invitar (invite), Tocar (touch)
Caminar (walk), Dejar (leave), Jugar (play), Tomar (take)
Cantar (sing), Escuchar (listen), Mirar (ide), Trabajar (work)
Cocinar (cook), Estudiar (study), Pintar (paint)
Comprar (buy), Hablar (talk), Preguntar (ask)

Regular -ER verb
Aprender (learn), Leer (read)
Beber (drink), Meter (put)
Comer (eat), Romper (broken)
Correr (run), Vender (sell)
Deber (must)

Regular -IR verb
Abrir (open), Partir (depart)
Añadir (add), Permitir (permit)
Compartir (share), Recibir (receive)
Decidir (decide), Vivir (live)
Dormir (sleep)

howismyspanish.com - version 2.1

to do within a reasonable amount of time. After debating with native Spanish speakers around the world it is safe to say that there are 7 tenses that are used on a daily basis, which is the reason we put together a blueprint. For anybody that feels they are ready for a next step in their Spanish learning journey:

Send an e-mail to hello@howismyspanish.com with the subject "SCC2989".

You will receive an automatic reply with a high definition Spanish conjugation blueprint PDF attached.

On the PDF you will find the most commonly used tenses in Spanish and the letters you should add behind the stem to form them.

Also highly recommended is;

https://howismyspanish.com/spanish-worksheets-for-beginners/

to download free worksheets to expand your vocabulary quickly.

References

Arias, E. (2021, May 14). *Verbos regulares e irregulares en español: explicación y lista de ejemplos.* Diccionario de Dudas. https://www.diccionariodedudas.com/verbos-regulares-e-irregulares/

Future with ir + a in Spanish Grammar. (n.d.). Lingolia Español. https://espanol.lingolia.com/en/grammar/tenses/futuro-proximo

Tiempos verbales en español: ¿Qué son y cuántos hay? (2019, September 19). Centro Estudios Cervantino. https://www.centroestudioscervantinos.es/tiempos-verbales-en-espanol/

Printed in Great Britain
by Amazon